THE EXCITING WORLD OF THE SLIME MOULDS

Bruce Ing

Visiting Professor of Environmental Biology

A Professorial Lecture
Delivered at the University of Chester
on 13 March 2003

Chester Academic Press

First published 2008
by Chester Academic Press
Corporate Communications
University of Chester
Parkgate Road
Chester CH1 4BJ

Printed and bound in the UK by the
LIS Print Unit,
University of Chester
Cover designed by the
LIS Graphics Team,
University of Chester

Text ©Bruce Ing, 2008
Images © the individual photographers

All Rights Reserved
No part of this publication may be reproduced, stored in a retrieval system or transmitted in any form or by any means without the prior permission of the copyright owner, other than as permitted by current UK legislation or under the terms of a recognised copyright licensing scheme

A catalogue record for this publication is available from the British Library

THE EXCITING WORLD OF THE SLIME MOULDS

Prologue

Slime moulds have been a major part of my life since 1957. As a first-year undergraduate at Cambridge, and already a keen field botanist, I visited the local Madingley Wood to collect mosses. Just inside the gate, I found a strange specimen, looking like a minute bunch of chestnut-coloured grapes, on the tips of the moss shoots. I carefully collected it and took it back to the Botany School, where no one was able to identify it! A few days later, I was browsing in the second-hand section of Heffers Bookshop and bought for 6d. a small booklet, published in 1909, about the models of Mycetozoa (as slime moulds were called then) in the Natural History Museum in South Kensington. There was a picture of my find, *Leocarpus fragilis*. I now knew the group, the name of my organism, and the names of the authors of the booklet, Arthur Lister and his daughter Gulielma. Back in the library, I soon found their 1925 monograph with beautiful coloured illustrations, not only of my *Leocarpus*, but of hundreds of other amazing looking objects. I was hooked! Since then, I have devoted most of my spare time to their study. As a student, I received little help and soon discovered that there were few people in Britain with an interest in them at any level. My main source of information came from workers in the United States and the Netherlands. Before long, I was in fruitful correspondence with people who were wonderfully generous with their knowledge and experience.

    Since those early days, I have been able to explore so many wonderful parts of the world in search of slime moulds and have made friends in all continents. They all share this excitement and sense of wonder, even after a lifetime of study. But what is it about slime moulds that are so exciting, and, first of all, what are they?

What are slime moulds?

Slime moulds were originally called Mycetozoa, or fungus-animals, because they were thought to lie somewhere between animals (or at least protozoans) and moulds (fungi). Nowadays, they seem best classified as part of the Kingdom Protozoa (which are *not* animals), but they are studied using methods appropriate to the Kingdom Fungi. There are two major groups (and a few smaller groups) of slime moulds, which may have a common ancestor, but are very different now.

1). **The cellular slime moulds**, or dictyostelids, have as a feeding stage a small amoeba-like organism that feeds on soil bacteria. Using chemical messengers, the cells communicate and aggregate into compact masses of thousands of cells which migrate in a slug-like form on to the soil surface. The cells retain their identity throughout, although they have different destinies. Some will form the building blocks of a stalk and then die, while the rest will swarm up the stalk and become spores. The spores will disperse and each can initiate a new colony elsewhere. There may be a sexual stage in the life cycle, but it is not morphologically separate.

2) **The plasmodial slime moulds,** which are the sort which I study, are called Myxomycetes, and are more complex. They have elaborate fruit-bodies containing spores which are formed by a reduction division (*meiosis*), so that the spores have only a half-set of chromosomes (they are

haploid). Later in the life-cycle, a fusion process restores the full chromosome set to the *diploid* state, and thus these slime moulds have sexual reproduction.

The **spores** are thick-walled, often ornamented with spines and ridges, and may remain viable for a century. On germination, a swarm-cell, or **myxoflagellate**, escapes and swims in water within the living or dead tissues of plants, or in the soil. This will depend on where the spore, which is either air- or insect-borne, lands. The swarm-cells divide to form large colonies of genetically identical individuals, or clones. Should the water content of the environment become less, the swarm-cells lose their flagella and becoming amoeboid. These **myxamoebae**, like the myxoflagellates, engulf bacteria, yeasts or small protozoans, and also divide to form large colonies. They are among the most abundant micro-organisms which occur in woodland, grassland and arable soil.

Myxamoebae act as gametes and fuse in genetically compatible pairs, producing a diploid **zygote**. There are three sexual strategies: the myxamoebae are of different mating types and must outbreed (*heterothallism*); they may be the same mating type (*homothallism*); or the myxamoebae proceed to the next stage without fusing (*agamism*). The first option ensures genetic variation in the next generation, but is less certain to happen; the second allows no variation, but is very reliable; while the last provides the student of myxomycetes with a great range of closely similar forms which are genetically distinct, rather like the situation in brambles, hawkweeds and dandelions among the flowering plants

Whichever strategy is adopted, the next stage is often spectacular. The zygote (or non-zygote myxamoeba in agamic species) undergoes massive non-reduction nuclear division (*mitosis*), without division of the rest of the cell. The resulting structure is a multinucleate **plasmodium**, often with millions of nuclei, and may grow to large size. The largest I have encountered, at Loggerheads, near Mold, was a metre square, two centimetres thick and probably weighed twenty kilograms. This has to be the largest single cell ever recorded! Usually, plasmodia are just a few centimetres in diameter and less than one millimetre thick. The plasmodium is not only a massive feeding structure, engulfing even fungal hyphae and fruit bodies, but is capable of rapid movement through water, soil, litter and dead wood. It also provides biologists with one of the best examples of protoplasmic streaming, *cyclosis,* where the granular cytoplasm streams within the vein-like strands of the plasmodium in one direction, then slows down, stops, reverses and speeds up in the opposite direction, and so on. This is an efficient cell transport system for the movement of nutrients in solution, but also, through the contraction and extension of microtubules, allows the whole structure to move.

When food supplies are used up, or as a response to so far unidentified internal timing mechanisms, the plasmodium migrates on to a suitable surface, such as soil, leaf litter, living plant stems or the surface of fallen wood, and transforms into the fruit-body stage. This may consist of anything from numerous simple stalked or un-stalked blobs a millimetre or so high to large masses in which the whole of the plasmodium has converted into a single spore mass. Meiosis occurs at spore formation (except in agamic species) and the life cycle is complete. When environmental conditions become unfriendly (too dry, too cold or too hot), the plasmodium may convert to a horn-like resting stage, the **sclerotium**, which revives when better conditions return.

The fruit body (**sporocarp**) may be a simple sac filled with spores (**sporocyst)**, either stalked or sessile, or a structure formed from the doily-like veins of the plasmodium as linear sporocarps, up to several centimetres long (at least twice as long as the typical diameter), but only one diameter wide (**plasmodiocysts**), or a structure made from the whole of the plasmodium heaped up in a domed mass several centimetres across. This last form can show the internal walls and stalks of what would have been component sporocysts (**pseudoaethalium**) or a continuous mass of spores and dispersal apparatus without any indication of component sporocysts (**aethalium**). As well as spores, most sporocarps contain a network, often loofah-like, of tubes, branched or otherwise, which contract in dry air and expand in moist air, thus allowing spores to be released into dry air, where they will be able to stay aloft longer.

Where do slime moulds live?

Most plasmodial slime moulds live in forest environments and are either based in dead wood or the leaf litter-soil interface. However, there are some important additional habitats which are of great ecological importance. Somewhat surprisingly, tropical rain forests are less rich in species than temperate woodlands, probably because of a combination of heavy rain, which destroys plasmodia and washes out of the soil both the food organisms and feeding stages of the slime moulds, and the rapid decomposition of both wood and litter in these forests, thus depriving the myxomycetes of their primary substrates. Nevertheless, there are several species which are only found in the tropics, in contrast to the majority, which are cosmopolitan.

Within the forest, there are several major habitats for myxomycetes. The first is the bark of living trees. Here, a group of highly specialised species live, almost exclusively. They are minute, usually too small to be seen with the naked eye, and their life cycle is often completed within one or two days. They appear to have adapted to drought conditions and their development is triggered by the wetting of the bark after rain. Many of these species have a reduced plasmodium, which does not move and in which streaming is also absent. It also produces but a single sporocyst. These minute species are easily detected, however, by culturing pieces of bark from living trees in moist chambers – Petri dishes kept moist with water and scanned on a daily basis for fruit bodies, with a stereomicroscope. In temperate environments, such as the British Isles and mainland Europe, myxomycetes have been isolated from 98% of all samples; they are clearly abundant in this habitat. In tropical forests, they are much less frequent, with perhaps only a 50-60% occurrence. This may be because of the smoothness of the bark of rain forest trees, which slows down the capture of air-borne spores, or simply the removal of the organisms by the rain.

Dead standing trees characteristically have a few species which are mostly found in that habitat, but the species are similar to those found on fallen wood. When the tree falls to the ground, its microclimate changes and is generally moister. As fungi decay the wood, it becomes a suitable environment for a large number of species of myxomycete. Some of these are typical of conifer wood, others are confined to hardwoods. The chemistry of the wood, especially its pH, is likely to be the prime factor, as it affects the diversity of potential food organisms for the slime moulds.

The accumulation of leaf litter and dead herbaceous stems on the woodland floor provides another prime habitat for myxomycetes, and many species are only found on these substrates. The type of litter, for example conifer needles or beech leaves, is discriminatory for several species and again leaf chemistry and pH are likely to be significant. Certain kinds of litter, such as holly, evergreen oak, olive or laurel, are slow to decay and form deep layers on the forest floor. In these situations, a number of characteristic assemblages of species, especially in Mediterranean woodlands, are found. Below beds of nettles or rosebay willow-herb, the soil is rich in phosphate and the dead stems of these plants are a fine substrate for the fruit bodies of myxomycetes. We now know that it is the myxoflagellates and myxamoebae, feeding on soil bacteria, which release the phosphate from digested bacterial cells and are therefore responsible for the increase in soil fertility.

On the walls and ledges of ravines where the wet rocks support a rich moss flora, a highly specialised group of myxomycetes occurs. They live in a kind of symbiosis with blue-green bacteria which fix both carbon and nitrogen from the atmosphere, a valuable trick in these nutrient-deficient sites. The myxomycete plasmodia have been found in close association with thalli of *Nostoc,* notably in the deep ravines of Snowdonia. In the moist Atlantic woods of the West of Scotland and the English Lake District, these species may also occur on boulders. Although the individual species have been found elsewhere, the ravine association itself has only been found in the British Isles.

A few species of myxomycete are typical of grassland and often occur on lawns and in sand dunes, as well as in chalk and limestone grassland. They are essentially soil organisms and simply crawl on to the grass, so that their spores are released into the air. Heathland and moorland are usually too acid for myxomycetes, but a few species have been found regularly associated with heather and bracken. Wetlands, especially those with a base-rich water supply, have a small suite of characteristic species, best seen in such places as the Norfolk Broads and the fenlands of Cambridgeshire. Acid bogs have one genuinely aquatic species, *Badhamia lilacina,* whose yellow plasmodium may be seen among submerged *Sphagnum* mosses before it converts into inconspicuous clumps of lilac-grey sporocysts on emergent vegetation.

Even coastal environments support a few species, although none have been found in temperate salt-marshes. A few woodland species are known from tropical mangrove swamps. However, the mats of vegetation on shingle beaches and the decaying grasses in sand dunes provide suitable sites for a number of species, although none are confined to this kind of habitat. The dung of herbivorous animals does, however, attract a large number of myxomycete species, many of them unknown from any other substrate. The dung of rabbit, donkey and deer is especially productive.

In the tropics, deserts and semi-deserts, as well as forests, contain a wide range of slime mould species, including soil and bark specialists; but the greatest interest lies in those species which inhabit the insides of rotting cactus stems and pads, as well as other succulents. The pads of the *Opuntia* species are rich in the American tropics and many of the slime mould species are also found on these hosts when they become naturalised in the Mediterranean region, including North Africa and the Canary Islands. In the latter area, they have also colonised the succulent spurges which are endemic to the archipelago. When a pad or stem is carefully opened, the sporocarps can often be found on the network of vascular tissue, surrounded by the pulp of the stem. The habitat is shared by the larvae of fruit flies (drosophilids) and there is evidence to suggest that the myxomycete spores are dispersed by the flies when they emerge. Several of the myxomycetes are unique to this habitat, but others are also found on decaying vegetation, especially that of grasses.

In another climatic extreme, our final ecological group takes us to the alpine and arctic regions of all the continents, including Antarctica. When the winter snowpack melts in the spring, the vegetation that has been flattened for at least three months is often covered with the sporocarps of an amazing range of beautiful species. The snow cover has prevented them from freezing and the melting snow has provided appropriate water supplies and, together with the spring sunshine, the conditions are suitable for their development. In the Alps and the Scottish Highlands, the receding snow patches are often fringed by new plant growth, which provides a good substrate for the fruit bodies. The same suite of species occurs in the mountains of North, Central and South America, Europe, Siberia, the Himalayan and Chinese regions, Japan, Australia, New Zealand and Antarctica. They have a very short season as fruit bodies; rain and wind remove them in a few days. On mountains, the updraft of warm air may lift the spores to the permanent snow-line and continually recycle the species in the alpine pastures, but we cannot say for certain – the research is yet to be done.

Why are slime moulds interesting?

To the biologist, slime moulds offer a range of fascinating topics for investigation and thought. Some are topics peculiar to the group, but many are models with a far wider significance. Slime moulds, many of which are easy to grow in culture, may therefore become inexpensive and instructive experimental organisms. None are known to produce toxins or allergens, so are safe to use in all kinds of laboratories.

To the ecologist, the main questions are concerned with the factors which determine where they are found. Food supply, especially the availability of suitable bacteria, is clearly important, as is temperature, rainfall and soil chemistry. Interaction with the vegetation and other organisms, especially insects, may be important. We have many questions, but few answers as yet.

To the geneticist and molecular biologist, they offer a wide range of reproductive strategies, an unusual plasticity in their *ploidy* (the number of complete chromosome sets in the nucleus), and a surprisingly high incidence of *introns* in the genome, more than nearly all other organisms. In addition, several genera, but especially *Didymium*, provide fuel for the long-running debate on biological and morphological species, where different morphologies may be seen in organisms which are genetically identical and identical morphologies may be shared by genetically distinct organisms. It may be confusing, but it *is* interesting.

To the chemist, they offer the challenge of a range of unique pigments which are not found in fungi and are similar to those in some insects, such as butterflies, and birds. In addition, these pigments are very difficult to extract.

To the evolutionist, they are also of great current interest and illustrate one of the more effective partnerships between molecular biology and traditional taxonomic methodology. They are not related to fungi, but share ancestry with soil protozoans such as amoeboflagellates, as seen by their fine structure and DNA. Within the wider groups of slime moulds, their phylogeny is slowly being pieced together and the relationships between families, for example, show some unexpected alliances. This provides for stimulating, exciting discussion between a wide range of biological disciplines.

To the developmental biologist, unique processes during spore formation are unlike those in any other organisms. The nature of their reproductive strategies raises interesting questions on the definition of what is an individual organism

Thus, what we do not yet know about slime moulds promises to be at least as interesting as what we *do* know.

The research potential of slime moulds

Molecular and genetic studies

This is a rapidly expanding area of interest for students of slime moulds and current and future work includes: the role of introns in the conversion of the genetic code, where myxomycetes are ideal models; studies on molecular phylogenies; and investigation of the differences between closely similar species, which needs molecular as well as classical taxonomy.

Medical uses

This is at present a small field of research, but has enormous potential. Some work has been started on using myxomycete plasmodia to study factors which affect the rate of nuclear division (of considerable significance in cancer research); work is also current on the role of enzymes derived from certain myxomycete plasmodia, which feed on fungi, for attacking fungal walls in deep-seated mycoses. It has long been known that myxomycete plasmodia produce novel antibiotics which are, at least, bacteriostatic, but little development work has taken place. An intriguing project involves the use of plasmodia to mop up bacteria in wounds and varicose ulcers (not unlike the use of maggots, but less nauseating). There is some potential for using myxoflagellates, myxamoebae and plasmodia as microfilms in vascular systems as scavengers and antibacterial agents.

Industrial uses
There is considerable potential in using plasmodia to clear bacterial microfilms in pipes, but no studies are yet in progress.

Agricultural uses
The most promising use of myxomycetes involves inoculating soils low in phosphate with species of *Didymium*, to increase the rate of release of phosphate in these soils.

Studies on climate change
There is now abundant evidence that Mediterranean and tropical species are moving northwards in the British Isles and mapping programmes have already started in the UK and other parts of Europe to chart their progress. There are clearly changes in alpine climates and it is hoped that monitoring the snowline species will allow the rate of change to become more accurately predictable.

Pollution studies
One of the simplest and most effective ways of monitoring changes in atmospheric pollution is the comparison of the population diversity and frequency of myxomycetes on the bark of living urban and rural trees. A good body of work has already been published on studies in London, with encouraging conclusions.

Bibliography

Ing, B. (1983). A ravine association of myxomycetes. *Journal of Biogeography, 10* (4), 299-306.

Ing, B. (1984). Myxomycetes in biology teaching. *Journal of Biological Education, 18* (4), 277-285.

Ing, B. (1994). The phytosociology of myxomycetes: Tansley review, no. 62. *New Phytologist, 126* (2), 175-201.

Ing, B. (1998a). Alpine myxomycetes in Scotland. *Botanical Journal of Scotland, 50* (1), 47-53.

Ing, B. (1998b). Corticolous myxomycetes from central London. *The London Naturalist, 77,* 83-89.

Ing, B. (1999). *The myxomycetes of Britain and Ireland: An identification handbook.* Slough, Richmond Publishing.

Ing, B. (2002). Corticolous myxomycetes from central London - 2. *The London Naturalist, 81,* 49-65.

Lister, A. (1909). *Guide to the British Mycetozoa exhibited in the Department of Botany, British Museum (Natural History)* (G. Lister, Ed.). (3rd ed.). London: British Museum. (Original work published 1895).

Lister, A. (1925). *A monograph of the Mycetozoa: A descriptive catalogue of the species in the Herbarium of the British*

Museum (G.Lister, Rev.). (3rd ed.). London: British Museum. (Original work published 1894).